For Ellis, Everett & Julien: thanks for the never-ending inspiration - LL

For my darling boys who keep me constantly creating - KB

Also Available

Copyright ©2021 by Liz Lynch & Katie Blauser
Published by PLP Publishing LLC
Illustrations by Liz Lynch
Design & photography by Katie Blauser
Printed in China

plppublishing.com

PANDAS LOVE PICKLES:
LET'S EAT!

Pandas Love Pickles, Pandas Love Pizza + Pandas Love Peas were created by Liz Lynch to help encourage young readers and picky eaters to explore new foods. The ABC books pair lifelike animals with silly foods they normally wouldn't try and inspire fun mealtime conversations and learning opportunities.

Pandas Love Pickles: Let's Eat! takes the trying experience even further by pairing each animal and food with a recipe or craft, playfully curated by Katie Blauser of Eat Pretty Darling. These activities bring the foods and crafts off the page and into your kitchen!

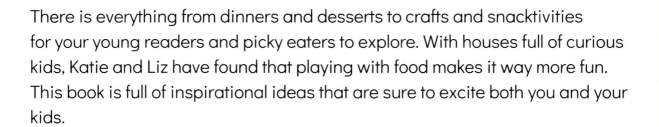

There is everything from dinners and desserts to crafts and snacktivities for your young readers and picky eaters to explore. With houses full of curious kids, Katie and Liz have found that playing with food makes it way more fun. This book is full of inspirational ideas that are sure to excite both you and your kids.

Try it, you might love it!

Please note that each recipe can be made gluten free by simply using a 1-to-1 substitution of gluten free all purpose flour and using other gluten free versions of the ingredients.

Aa

Aardvarks try alphabet soup

Ingredients

- 1 tablespoon olive oil
- 1 clove garlic, minced
- ½ small sweet onion, diced
- 2 teaspoons Italian seasoning
- ½ teaspoon salt
- 8 cups vegetable broth
- 1 lb. frozen mixed vegetables (corn, carrots, peas, green beans)
- 8 oz. can tomato sauce
- 2 cups alphabet pasta

STILL NOT SURE ABOUT SOUP? Serve it with a straw and try drinking it!

Prep time: 5 minutes
Cook time: 15 minutes
Makes: 8 cup servings

ABC SOUP

Directions

1. In a large pot over medium heat add olive oil, garlic, onion, Italian seasoning, and salt. Stir occasionally and cook until onions turn translucent, about 5 minutes.

2. Turn the heat to high and add in vegetable broth, frozen vegetables, and tomato sauce. Bring to a boil and add in pasta. Cook noodles in the soup according to pasta box directions. Serve immediately.

Bb
Bears try beets

Ingredients

- ½ cup beet puree (about 1 medium beet)
- 1 tablespoon olive oil for roasting beet
- 2 eggs
- ¼ cup maple syrup
- ¼ cup sugar
- ¼ cup milk
- ¼ cup coconut oil, melted
- 1 cup all purpose flour
- ½ cup unsweetened cocoa powder
- ¼ teaspoon salt
- 1 teaspoon baking soda
- ½ cup chocolate chips

To make bear

- 12 mini marshmallows
- 24 mini chocolate chips
- 12 blueberries
- 2 bananas

Prep time: 60 minutes
Cook time: 22 minutes
Makes: 12 muffins

CHOCOLATE BEET MUFFINS

Directions

1. Preheat the oven to 400°F. Remove the stem and any roots from the beets. Scrub them well under running water to remove any dirt. Drizzle the beets with olive oil and wrap tightly in foil. Place on a baking sheet and bake for one hour or until the beets are tender and a knife is easily inserted.

2. After the beets are done cooking, place them in a bowl and let cool in the fridge. Once the beets are cool, rub the outside of the beet to remove the skin or peel with a knife. Place the beets in a food processor and pulse until a puree is created.

3. Preheat the oven to 375°F and line a muffin tin with paper liners or grease it well.

4. In a large bowl, combine the beet puree, eggs, maple syrup, sugar, milk, and oil. Whisk and set aside.

5. In a small bowl mix together the flour, cocoa powder, salt, and baking soda. Gradually add the dry ingredients to the wet ingredients and whisk well after each addition.

6. Once you have fully combined the wet and dry ingredients, stir in the chocolate chips. Scoop the batter into your prepared muffin tin and fill each cup ¾ full. Bake for 20-22 minutes. Remove from the oven and let cool before decorating.

7. **To make bear:**
(Wait to decorate until ready to serve to keep bananas fresh) Cut bananas into ¼ inch round slices. Next, cut 12 of the banana slices in half and place them on the top sides of each muffin for ears. Place one full circle slice on the bottom middle of each muffin for the snout.

8. Cut a mini marshmallow in half and place the sticky side down on the muffin on the top side of the full banana slice. Stick a mini chocolate chip on top of each marshmallow half to make eyes. Place a blueberry on top of the full banana circle for the nose. Store in an air tight container in the fridge.

Cc
Chickens try chickpeas

Ingredients

- 1 can chickpeas, drained and rinsed well
- ½ cup natural peanut butter
- 2 teaspoons vanilla extract
- ⅛ teaspoon salt
- ⅛ teaspoon baking soda
- ¼ cup pure maple syrup
- ½ cup rolled oats
- ½ cup semi-sweet chocolate chips
- sprinkles (optional)

DID YOU KNOW? Chickpeas are also called Garbanzo Beans.

Prep time: 10 minutes
Makes: about 2 cups

EDIBLE CHICKPEA COOKIE DOUGH

Directions

1. Add all of the ingredients to a food processor except for the chocolate chips. Process until it forms a smooth dough, this may take a while! Scrape down the sides if needed as you puree.

2. Once the dough is formed, stir in the chocolate chips by hand. Add in any other favorite cookie toppings and roll into balls or enjoy the cookie dough straight with a spoon!

3. Store in an airtight container in the fridge for up to 5 days.

Dd
Dolphins try donuts

Ingredients

- ½ cup milk
- 1 egg
- 1 teaspoon vanilla extract
- ⅓ cup sugar
- ¼ cup coconut oil, melted
- 1 cup flour
- 1 teaspoon baking powder
- ¼ teaspoon salt

Glaze

- 1 cup powdered sugar
- 2 tablespoons milk
- 1 drop of blue food coloring

NO DONUT TRAY?
Make tin foil cylinders and stick in the middle of each cup of a muffin tin.

Prep time: 10 minutes
Cook time: 10 minutes
Makes: 8 donuts

BAKED VANILLA DONUTS

Directions

1. Preheat the oven to 425°F and grease donut trays. In a medium bowl mix the milk, egg, sugar, vanilla, and oil together with a whisk.

2. In a small bowl, stir together the flour, baking powder, and salt. Gradually add the dry mix to the wet, mixing well after each addition. Whisk until there are no lumps. Spoon into the donut pan and fill three quarters full. Bake for 8-10 minutes or until cooked through.

3. While they are baking, make the glaze. To make the glaze, mix all of the glaze ingredients together with a whisk and set aside. Remove the donuts from the oven and let cool completely.

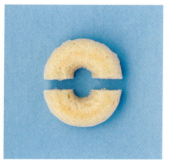

Cut the donut in half. Set one half aside and take the other half and cut the sides off. You will have one square left in the middle, cut that diagonally across to create two triangles.

5. Place one of the cut sides on the top middle part of the uncut donut half as the fin. Take the other cut side and one of the triangles and place them on the left end of the uncut donut half to make a tail.

6. Set the donuts on a cooling rack and pour the glaze over top to make the donut pieces stick together. Add a mini chocolate chip eye if desired.

Ee

Elephants try eggs

Ingredients

- 6 eggs
- 4 oz. cream cheese, cubed
- 1 tablespoon unsalted butter

LOW AND SLOW
The key is cooking the eggs very slowly over low heat.

Prep time: 2 minutes
Cook time: 8 minutes
Makes: 4 servings

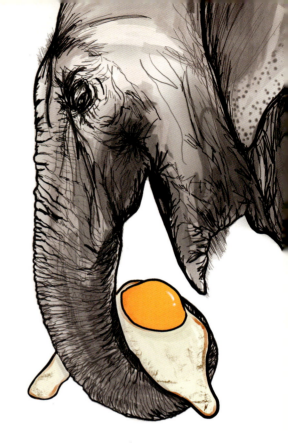

THE BEST SCRAMBLED EGGS

Directions

1. Crack the eggs into a medium bowl. Whisk them very well until no separation of egg yolk and whites. Mix in the cream cheese and stir.

2. Heat a pan on low heat and add the butter to coat the bottom of the pan. Add in the egg mixture and continuously stir over low heat. Soft curds will begin to form and the cream cheese will melt. Remove the eggs from the heat when done and serve immediately.

Ff

Flamingos try figs

Supplies

- 4 wood beads
- 8 pink feathers
- 4 pink pipe cleaners
- Black paint
- Hot glue
- 4 paper straws

Craft time: 15 minutes
Makes: 4 flamingos

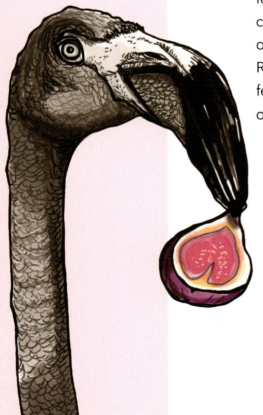

FLAMINGO STRAW

Directions

1. Warm up the glue gun and sit the wood bead on a table with the hole side down. Put a dot of glue on the top side of the wood bead towards the hole. Stick the end of the feather into it and let it cool.

2. Put another dot of hot glue on the side of the bead, wrap the feather around and carefully push it down onto the bead. Repeat with the other feather on the opposite side.

3. Cut your pipe cleaners in half and start to tie a loose knot on one end of the pipe cleaner. Let it stay loose to look like the head. Curve the rest of the pipe cleaner like an S making the tied end the head. Dip the tip of the pipe cleaner poking out from the head into black paint to make it look like the beak. Let it dry completely.

4 Put a dot of hot glue on the top of the wood bead right next to the top hole. Stick the bottom part of the pipe cleaner (opposite side from the head) into the hot glue and let the pipe cleaner stick into the hole of the bead. Repeat steps with all of your wood beads. Slide your flamingo onto a straw and you're ready to have a fancy flamingo drink!

Gg

Gorillas try granola bars

Ingredients

- 1 cup creamy peanut butter
- ½ cup maple syrup
- 3 cups old fashioned oats

NO PEANUTS, NO PROBLEM!
Any nut butter will work for these yummy bars.

Prep time: 10 minutes
Freeze time: 30 minutes
Makes: 12 bars

PEANUT BUTTER GRANOLA BARS

Directions

1. Line a baking sheet with parchment paper. Heat the peanut butter and maple syrup in a saucepan over medium heat stirring constantly until it comes just to a boil.

2. Add the oats to the peanut butter mixture and stir until combined. Pour the oats into the lined baking dish and spread evenly. Press it firmly together with a spatula so it sticks together.

3. Put the pan into the freezer for 30 minutes or until set. Remove the bars from the pan by lifting the parchment paper and use a large knife to slice it in half long ways and then into 1.5 inch bars. Store in an airtight container in the refrigerator until ready to eat.

Hh

Hippos try hamburgers

Ingredients

- 1 lb. ground beef
- 1 teaspoon salt
- ½ teaspoon ground black pepper
- 6 slices of cheddar cheese
- 6 popsicle sticks
- Cookie cutter (optional)

SERVE IT ON A STICK!
From veggie to turkey burgers, try this with any burger.

Prep time: 10 minutes
Cook time: 15 minutes
Makes: 5 slider burgers

HAMBURGER POPS

Directions

1. Prepare your hamburgers by dividing the ground beef into 6 equal portions. Form them into a small patty and sprinkle the outside with salt and pepper. Keep them slider size, about 2 inches across, so that they easily fit on a popsicle stick without being too big.

2. Cook the burgers in a hot pan or on the grill for 3-4 minutes on each side or until desired doneness.

3. Remove from the grill and place slices of cheese on top of the burger and let them cool slightly. To make cheese designs, use a small cookie cutter to cut out cheese shapes and place them on the burger once it has cooled.

4. Place the burger on the popsicle stick by inserting it on one of the ends. Serve along with favorite dips!

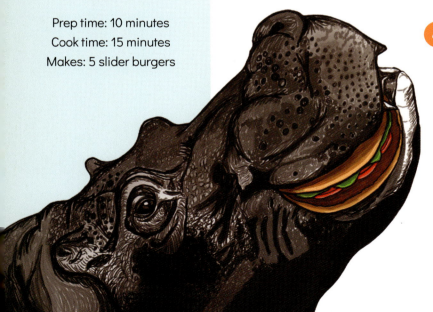

Ii

Iguanas try ice cream

Ingredients

- 4 cups powdered sugar
- 16 oz. can white frosting
- Food coloring

TASTE SAFE
This play dough is taste safe although it won't taste too yummy!

Craft time: 5 minutes

ICE CREAM PLAY DOUGH

Directions

1. Add 1 cup of powdered sugar to the bottom of a large bowl. Next, add 10-20 drops of food coloring into the frosting container and mix well. Put the frosting into the bowl of powdered sugar and stir together with a spatula.

2. Gradually add the remaining 3 cups of powdered sugar, mixing well with each addition until it forms a play dough consistency or dough is no longer sticky.

Jj
Jellyfish try jam

Ingredients
- 2 cups frozen (or fresh) raspberries
- 2 tablespoons chia seeds
- 1-2 tablespoons honey or maple syrup

To make jellyfish
- Assorted sizes rickrack
- Googly eyes
- Glue

Prep time: 10 minutes
Cook time: 15 minutes
Makes: 2 cups
Craft time: 30 minutes

RASPBERRY CHIA JAM

Directions

1. Place the unopened bag of frozen raspberries from the freezer into the fridge overnight. In the morning, squish around the bag to break up the pieces keeping it sealed so it doesn't spill out. If you're using fresh, skip this step.

2. Add the raspberries, chia seeds and honey into a medium bowl. Mix it all together until combined. If using fresh raspberries, use a fork to lightly mash them.

3. Take a taste and add additional honey if needed depending on berry sweetness. Pour the jam into a jar or airtight container and store in the fridge for up to a week.

4. **To make the jellyfish:**
Cut 6 inch long pieces of assorted sized rickrack. About 6 pieces will do but more can be added for a fuller look. Criss cross the rickrack across the round metal lid of the jar. Add a dot of glue each time a piece is added layering them on top of one another. Let dry flat.

CRAFT & COOK

5 Glue the googly eyes to the side of the silver ring of the jar. Let dry completely. After adding your jam to the jar, place the metal lid on top of the jar and screw the metal ring around on top of the rickrack pieces so it holds them down.

Kk

Kangaroos try kiwi

Ingredients

- 2 cups mango
- 1 banana
- 1 cup yogurt
- ½ cup orange juice
- Juice of one lime
- 1 kiwi, peeled and sliced into circles

MAKE IT A SMOOTHIE!
Skip the popsicle mold and enjoy it as a drink.

Prep time: 15 minutes
Freeze Ttme: 8+ hours
Makes: 8 large popsicles

TROPICAL KIWI POPSICLES

Directions

1. Add the mango, banana, yogurt, orange juice, and lime juice to a blender. Blend until it becomes a smooth liquid.

2. Pour the mixture into a popsicle mold and place popsicle sticks. Put the tray into the freezer and let harden.

Ll

Lions try lasagna

Ingredients

- 1 box rotini noodles
- 1 jar spaghetti sauce
- 8 oz. ricotta cheese
- 2 cups shredded mozzarella cheese
- ½ cup shredded parmesan cheese

To make lion

- Slice cheddar cheese
- Slice provolone cheese
- Red pepper
- Black olive slices

Prep time: 15 minutes
Cook time: 25 minutes
Makes: 8 servings

LAZY LASAGNA

Directions

1. Preheat the oven to 375°F and pour ¼ cup of the spaghetti sauce into the bottom of a 13x9 casserole dish.

2. Boil the rotini as directed on the box for the shortest suggested time to make them al dente. Drain the pasta and pour half of the noodles on top of the spaghetti sauce in the casserole dish.

3. Dollop spoonfuls of ricotta cheese on top of the noodles. Sprinkle 1 cup of the mozzarella on top of the ricotta and pour on 1 cup of the spaghetti sauce. Add the rest of the noodles and top with remaining spaghetti sauce.

4. Sprinkle the remaining mozzarella and parmesan cheese on the top. Bake uncovered for 20-25 minutes or until the cheese has melted and gets bubbly and golden brown on top.

5 **To make the lion:**
Use a large round cookie cutter to make a circle with the cheddar cheese. Use a small round cookie cutter to cut one circle and then cut in half for the ears. Use a small round cookie cutter to make two small circles and one half circle with the provolone cheese. Cut a small wide triangle out of the red pepper. Lay the large cheddar circle in the middle of the plate and add the pasta around the outside.

6 Lay the bottom half circle just below the large circle with the flat side facing towards the large circle. Lay the two small circles on top of the others at the bottom towards the half circle. Place the pepper nose on top of the small circles and two olive slice eyes above the nose. Add the ears to each side of the top of the plate.

Mm

Meerkats try mango

Ingredients

- 2 cups frozen mango
- 1 cup yogurt (plain, vanilla, or Greek)

Prep time: 10 minutes
Makes: 4 servings

MANGO FROZEN YOGURT

Directions

1 Add mango and yogurt to the food processor. Let it sit for 5 minutes for the mango to soften up a bit. Pulse the food processor and scrape down the sides when needed until it becomes a creamy consistency and no chunks left.

2 Once it resembles a soft frozen yogurt you can enjoy immediately or spread it evenly in the bottom of a loaf pan and place in the freezer for 3 hours for a firmer consistency. When going to scoop out of the freezer, let it sit out on the counter for 5-10 minutes to soften and be able to scoop.

FRUITY FUN!
Use any frozen fruit to make different flavors.

Nn

Narwhals try noodles

Supplies

- 1 box spaghetti pasta
- 20 drops blue food coloring
- Plastic ocean toys
- Chopsticks (optional)

DON'T BE BLUE! Turning blue? Rinse the noodles off after coloring them.

Craft Time: 15 minutes

NOODLE SENSORY BIN

Directions

1. Boil your pasta according to package directions. Drain well and let the noodles cool completely.

2. In a large plastic bag, add in the noodles and food coloring and squish the food coloring around until it coats all of the pasta. Pour the colored noodles into a plastic bin and add plastic ocean toys.

3. Pretend to be a narwhal and use a chopstick to explore through the bin to find the other animals. Store noodles in an airtight bag in the fridge for up to 3 days.

Oo

Octopus try oatmeal

Ingredients

- 1 cup water
- 1 cup blueberries
- 1 cup rolled oats
- 1 cup milk
- 2-4 tablespoons maple syrup

To make octopus
- Banana
- Blueberries

Prep time: 5 minutes
Cook time: 15 minutes
Makes: 2 servings

BLUEBERRY OATMEAL

Directions

1. Bring the water to a boil over high heat in a medium size saucepan. Turn the heat to medium low and add the blueberries. Simmer until the blueberries begin to burst, about 3 minutes.

2. Next, add in the oats and simmer for another 5 minutes. Add in the milk and maple syrup and stir. Cook for 5 more minutes. Serve warm.

3. **To make the octopus:** Cut two slices of banana and place in the middle of the bowl. Place two blueberries on each eye and create eight legs around the bowl.

Pp
Pandas try pickles

Supplies
- Paper plate
- Black construction paper
- Scissors
- Black marker
- Glue stick
- Tape
- Wide wood craft stick

Craft time: 10 minutes

PAPER PLATE PANDA

Directions

1. Take a plain white paper plate and cut off the bottom quarter. Cut two circles in the middle for eye holes.

2. Use a black marker to draw long ovals around the eye circles and out to the side. Draw a triangle nose below the eyes with a line going down that goes out to each side for the mouth.

3. Cut two semi circles out of black construction paper. Use the glue stick to glue the black construction paper ears on top to the back of the paper plate so that they stick out.

4. Tape the wide wood craft stick to the back of the paper plate on one side so the panda face can be held up as a mask. Pretend to be a panda and try some pickles!

CRAFT TIME

QUICK PICKLES
1 cucumber, thinly sliced
1 ½ cups vinegar
½ cup water
Salt + Pepper
Add cucumbers, vinegar, water, salt + pepper to a jar. Keep covered in the refrigerator for up to one week.

Qq

Quail try quesadillas

Ingredients

- ¼ cup hummus
- 1 cup shredded cheddar cheese
- 4 tortillas
- Cookie cutter

STICKING TO THE PAN? Add a small amount of oil or butter to the pan before cooking.

Prep time: 5 minutes
Cook time: 5 minutes
Makes: 4 servings

CHEESE + HUMMUS QUESADILLA

Directions

1. Spread a thin layer of 1 tablespoon of the hummus on one half of the tortilla. Sprinkle about a quarter cup of cheese on top of the hummus.

2. Fold the tortilla in half to sandwich the cheese and hummus and put in a hot pan over medium heat. Toast until golden brown, flip and toast the other side.

3. Cut the tortilla in half to make two triangles. Use a cookie cutter to cut shapes out of the triangles.

Rr

Rabbits try rice

Ingredients

- 2 tablespoons olive oil
- 2 tablespoons minced sweet onion
- 1 clove garlic, minced
- 2 cups white or brown rice, cooked
- 1 cup frozen cauliflower rice
- 1 cup frozen peas and carrots
- 2 eggs
- 3 tablespoons soy sauce or coconut aminos
- 1 tablespoon butter

Prep time: 5 minutes
Cook time: 10 minutes
Makes: 4 servings

VEGGIE FRIED RICE

Directions

1. Add oil to a pan over medium heat and stir in onion and garlic. Cook until onions become soft and add in the frozen vegetables and cook for 2 minutes.

2. Move the veggies to the side and crack the eggs onto the other side of the pan. Quickly scramble it with your spatula and keep moving it around until cooked.

3. Add the cauliflower rice and cook for 2 minutes. Now stir in the rice (if using frozen rice, add it when adding cauliflower rice), soy sauce, and butter.

4. Turn the heat up to medium high and mix the rice around letting it get a little golden brown.

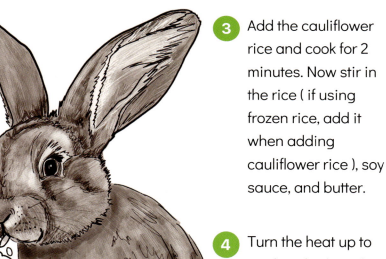

CAULI-POWER!
Pack a veggie punch by using just cauliflower rice.

Ss
Sloth try spinach

Ingredients

- 2 ripe bananas
- 2 cups rolled oats
- Handful of spinach
- ½ cup semi-sweet chocolate chips

BROWN BANANAS
The more ripe the banana the sweeter the cookies will be!

Prep time: 10 minutes
Cook time: 20 minutes
Makes: 14 cookies

SPINACH + BANANA COOKIES

Directions

1. Preheat the oven to 375°F and line a baking sheet. Place the banana and spinach in a blender and puree until the banana is liquified. Mix in the oats and chocolate chips by hand.

2. Scoop into a ball and place onto the prepared baking sheet 1 inch apart. Bake for 20 minutes and let cool for 5 minutes before removing from the pan.

Tt

Turtles try tacos

Ingredients
- 1 lb. chicken breast, sliced into 1 inch strips
- 3 bell peppers, seeds removed and sliced into strips
- 1 package taco seasoning
- 2 tablespoons olive oil

To make turtle
- Avocado
- Crunchy corn tortilla

Prep time: 10 minutes
Cook time: 25 minutes
Makes: 8 tacos

SHEET PAN TACOS

Directions

1. Preheat the oven to 425°F. Place the peppers and chicken on a sheet pan and drizzle with oil. Sprinkle the packet of taco seasoning over the chicken and peppers and use clean hands to rub the seasoning around and coat each piece.

2. Spread the chicken and peppers out so that it's all in one layer and bake in the oven for 22-25 minutes or until the chicken reaches an internal temperature of 160°F. Serve with salsa, cheddar cheese, sour cream, avocado, or any favorite taco toppings.

3. **To make turtle:**
Cut the avocado into slices and lay two on top of each other and cut in half. Place on the bottom of a crunchy tortilla as the legs. Cut a circle out of the avocado and place at the front of the taco.

Uu

Unicorns try ube

Ingredients

- 1 ube (purple sweet potato), peeled and cubed
- 4 cups water
- 1 cup fresh squeezed lemon juice
- ½ cup honey

Prep time: 10 minutes
Cook time: 20 minutes
Makes: 6 cups

MAGIC UBE LEMONADE

Directions

1. Place 2 cups of water in a saucepan and add the potatoes. Bring to a boil until the potatoes are fork tender, about 10-15 minutes. Drain the boiling liquid into a pitcher and set the potatoes aside. Pour the potato water into an ice cube tray and freeze until set.

2. In a pitcher, mix together the other two cups of water, honey, and lemon juice. Stir until the honey has dissolved.

3. Once the ice cubes are frozen, place them in a glass and pour the lemon water over the ice cubes and watch the colors change. Sip and enjoy!

DID YOU KNOW?
Ube is the same thing as a purple sweet potato.

Vv

Vultures try vegetables

Ingredients
- Vegetables
- Dips

NOT READY TO TASTE? Use other senses like touch and smell to explore the food.

Prep time: 10 minutes

VEGETABLE TRY TRAY

Directions

1. Use an ice cube tray or muffin tin to put an assortment of veggies and dips. Have a taste test and compare the veggies. Take notes!

2. Here are some questions to use:
   What color is each vegetable?
   Is it crunchy or soft?
   Does it taste sweet or bitter?
   Which one tasted best in which dip?
   Do the colors taste different?

Ww

Whales try waffles

Ingredients

- 1 ½ cups flour
- 2 teaspoons baking powder
- ½ teaspoon salt
- 1 cup milk
- 2 eggs
- 1 teaspoon vanilla extract
- 2 tablespoons maple syrup
- 2 tablespoons butter, melted

To make whale

- Blueberries
- Strawberry
- Mini marshmallow
- Mini chocolate chip
- Yogurt

FREEZER FRIENDLY
Lay waffles flat to freeze and store in a freezer bag.

Prep time: 10 minutes
Cook time: 2 minutes each
Makes: 10 small waffles

WAFFLES

Directions

1. In a medium bowl, whisk together the flour, baking powder, and salt. Add in the milk, eggs, vanilla, maple syrup, and butter, and stir until just combined. Scoop the batter into a warmed waffle iron and cook until golden brown.

2. **To make whale:**
Cut the waffle in half. Cut a triangle out of the other half and put on one end of the half waffle to make the tail.

3. Place blueberries under the whale for water. Cut a sliver of strawberry for the mouth. Cut a mini marshmallow in half for the eye and top it with a mini chocolate chip.

4. Fill a plastic bag with yogurt and snip the end. Squirt elongated dots on top of the whale to make the spout.

Xx

X-ray fish try everything

Supplies

- ¼ cup Water
- 2 drops black food coloring
- Paper
- White crayon
- Paintbrush

WATERCOLORS WORK
Don't have black food coloring? Use watercolor paints!

X-RAY PAINTING

Directions

1. Mix the black food coloring into the water to make your water paint.

2. Draw a fish on a piece of paper with a white crayon. You won't be able to see what it is! Brush the black water paint over the crayon drawing to reveal the x-ray.

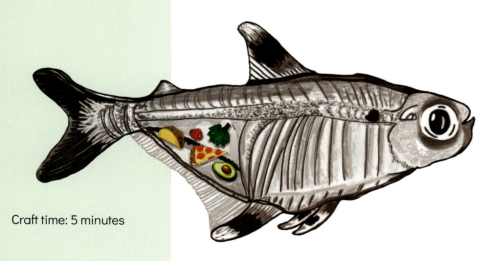

Craft time: 5 minutes

Yy

Yaks try yogurt smoothies

Ingredients

- 1 frozen banana
- ¼ cup frozen cauliflower (cooked and then frozen)
- 2 tablespoons peanut butter (or any nut butter)
- 1 tablespoon unsweetened cocoa powder
- 1 cup milk

Prep time: 10 minutes
Makes: 2 smoothies

50

YUMMY YOGURT SMOOTHIE

Directions

1. Add all of the ingredients into a blender. Pulse until it becomes creamy and there are no chunks left.

2. Pour into a cup and drink cold.

Zz

Zebras try zucchini

Ingredients

- 2 cups shredded zucchini
- 1 cup vegetable oil
- 1 cup granulated sugar
- 3 eggs
- 2 cups flour
- ¼ teaspoon salt
- ½ teaspoon baking powder
- ½ teaspoon baking soda
- 1 teaspoon cinnamon
- 2 tablespoons unsweetened cocoa powder

Prep time: 15 minutes
Cook Time: 60 minutes
Makes: 1 loaf

CHOCOLATE SWIRL ZUCCHINI BREAD

Directions

1. Preheat the oven to 350°F and grease a loaf pan.

2. In a large bowl, mix together the zucchini, oil, sugar, and eggs. Gradually add in the flour, salt, baking powder, cinnamon, and baking soda. Stir until just combined and divide the batter in half and put one half in a separate bowl.

3. Add the cocoa powder to one of the bowls and mix until just combined. Pour some of the non-chocolate batter into the bottom of the loaf pan, it doesn't need to be even. Next add some of the chocolate batter.

4. Use a butter knife to swirl the two batters together slightly. Add the remaining batters to the pan and use the knife again to swirl the two batters together. Bake for 45-60 minutes or until cooked through.

PREFER MUFFINS? Make muffins instead and cook for 22-24 minutes.